Moving On:

Poems by

Kathleen Bartholomew

I dedicate this book to-:

My grandsons, James and Joe, whom I love so much.

'Remember also your Creator in the days of your youth'
Eccl. 12:1 RSV

First published in 2010 by lulu.com

A CIP catalogue record for this book is available from the British Library.

ISBN (paperback) 978-1-4467-2446-0

Acknowledgements to publishers

Dover
Forward Press, Remus House Coltsfoot Drive
Northampton PE2 9JX
Anthology entitled 'Inspired Minds' July 2010
Last Goodbyes
Forward Press, Remus House, Woodston, Peterborough PE2 9JX
Anthology entitled 'Far and Wide' 31st May 2010
Begin Again
Forward Press, Remus House, Woodston, Peterborough PE2 9JX
Anthology entitled 'My Words Are My Voice' 31st December 2009
Moving On
Sheltered Times Ashfield District Council
Urban Road, Kirkby in Ashfield Notts October 2008
Might It Not Be
Poetry Now, subsidiary of Forward Press
Woodston Peterborough PE2 9JX October 2006
Included in -
'Midland and East Anglia Poets'
part of Forward Press, Woodston Peterborough PE2 9JX:
24th November 2006
Welcome Home
Poetry Now,
part of Forward Press. Woodston Peterborough PE2 9JX
anthology entitled 'Poppy Fields' September 2007
Uncompromised
Exile, 'Poems to print'
John Marr, Exile, 8 Snow Hill, Clare, Suffolk. 16th December 2004

Contents

Begin again

Sun loungers stacked in sixes
like white wiggly worms mating,
wait alongside faded boats
cocked to one side.

Four young girls in hooded jacket tops
stop and pose
on the deserted soft, sandy beach,
waiting to be directed by the camera man
and his crew, arriving,
waving his arms, wearing a red shirt.

A lone child runs from the teasing tide,
as it laps upon the beach
and recedes,
her feet and ankles wet,
she shouts with glee.
A stinging jelly-fish floats in aimlessly.

The cranes on the hillside overlook the bay;
working all day to build more holiday flats.
The established buildings look and yawn,
their portals wide, wait,
then wake. when the summer sun shines inside.

The council cart drops the blue bins
along the promenade,
lined with white plastic bags, prepared,
to be filled with discarded food and drink wrappers.

- his hammer thuds, echoing
across the bay, driving in the stakes
that hold the umbrellas.
The empty chairs put out- wait,
the restaurant's sheltered shutters slide apart –
tomorrow the season will start.

Past, present, future, no more

The past has gone,
nothing can be done to change that;

we can, in retrospect move on
from ages that we wore, like a badge.

The past becomes the present.
We are responsible for making it the future.

Decisions- steps forward,
open doors, new loves, lives shared.

Building towards happiness
as a cure for life- as difficult as it is,

when a Lot philosophy hounds us.
Do we sit and watch the city burn down?

We may move towards the next goal,
knowing what we do is right;

if we act from the very soul of what we are
and fight those demons. In truth there is a future.

A year without one of the seasons
would leave an awful gap, so …

Cuspids

Hello! It's me.
I'm back,
back from seeing Daniel.
I showed him the cage where I was.
I told him about the show I gave
and how the people loved it-
I said,
I made a photo shoot of canines bared,
how I faced and stared
between the jaws of death
and smiled again and again.
he loved it and he smiled too.
I told him,
it's easier when the path was trod before,
nobody would believe me,
but he did,
he said
It wasn't me-
the lions had been fed,
they were not hungry anymore.

He had a nasty scar where the wound had healed,
I could see it staring through his shirt.
he shrugged.

I said,
I know that the scars don't go away.
He said,
I'll remember that.
I said.
Hello! Is any body there? I'm back.

A thirsty kill

From the highest hill
hovering down the valley
walking clouds-
dispersing rain
onto favoured spots
(some stay dry)

moving like steered fog
extinguished
by the sun's later rays
drinking it
sinks
drunkenly
beyond the horizon
ending of the day.

Demons

Work hard to be free
of the spell that binds you.
Never think for a moment
that you are different to me.

I may be the one that is stronger now!

but there was a time when
I was almost taken away
and this enables me,
to look after you today.

Time and Place

Red Geraniums
flooding the patio:
Water sprinkler tends the thirsty lawn
with finger fist.
The pumped fountain trickles
down and back,

The contorted willow's
tender green leaves,
on rich brown branches
twist and turn and twist.
… a telephone rings.

The birds are all in bed,
waiting for the dawn-
to sing their feathered song.
The eucalyptus tree
oozes odours into the opening night.
A hub of voices listen.

The b b q grill,
warm with embers
fire and spark into the evening light.
The throb of music
winds down, softly,
ending the deep purple day.

It's here

The streets and pavements are lined with gold
copper coins flicked and picked up by the wind -a winner.
Prickly hedgehogs are hibernating, insulating hide-aways.
Squirrels storing hoards of hazelnuts in lofty trees.
The gales and rains are here again to blow away the blues
and greys of the fast moving yonder winter skies.
Time for long nights and shorter days.
Dick Whittington and his cat are here at last and in the news;
caught and sentenced for shoplifting,
drifting, knee deep in leaves, lying on park benches.
Him in harmony with the gold, yellows, and greens,
of the great autumn concert.
To the_country of origin we vow, English produce,
Victoria, Conference and Cox's, best, we've seen
pantomime extremes fit for a queen.

Round about me

Mare and foal running free
in an adjacent meadow field.
Her white main flowing as she dances,
the colt prances after her.

Beyond, the M1 intrudes-
bringing to life the last of the busy working day,
the lorries groan and drone on home,
some homeless,
coloured cars zip by,

going home to their kids,
the wife, the mate,
some to sadness, some to bliss.
Except for truth and lies, our lives are like this
mare and foal running free.

A Bed of Nails

Aided by a bed fit to fly to a new world.
Curly Locks cushions, salubrious throws.
Leather headboard, smooth, sturdy, to lean on-
where none went before (only a broken fitting).

Spongy pillows, a quilt of down.
I dare hardly lay my head.
I shake with surprise- *is this for me?*
Four smiling angels- faces tear stained,
tired, pull me there.

Gone is the old flat battered mattress
and underlying board
that in the past
nursed a couple of disintegrated discs.
The births it bore. The trashed lives,
the sins and forgiveness left unclaimed.

Old and damaged,
no one cared to replace-
it's all gone now
a new healing begins,
a recovery, a return

home from hospital,
thankful for my life at last,
my damaged body cut open
and the cancer robbed of life.

Deft the surgeon's knife,
A man of his word-
promises a few more years
to begin again, on a new bed of life.

Welcome Home

He went to join up when he was sixteen
because it was the done thing.
Your Country Needs You.
So he left his work, his family, his band and friends.
He went to no-mans-land.

Sally said they didn't know him when he came home
from World War 1.
He was dirty, ill, dehydrated and weighed 6 stones.
Lice crawling out of his shoe lace holes, and an unfamiliar smell.
So he had to stay outside while they bathed him on the yard.
Got him some clothes, shoes with soles. -Welcome Home.

He had been left alone-to die in the trenches, with the leeches.
Gassed and shell shocked by the Jerry bombs.
He was taken to a place to be treated for his tremors.
Sally said, the place was appalling so she brought him home-
to care for him.-Welcome Home.

In his box of belongings there was a pair of ear rings
which belonged to a mademoiselle in France-
Black ebony, three tiered balls,
with rings of gold around, to enhance them.
Oh, and his medals, there were three.

The worn Hohner harmonica he used as soap- to bathe his soul.
A diary, the pages white with brown edges.
He recorded his days in the trenches through drawings.
He hadn't learned to write; education wasn't free.
Inside was a sketch of his mother, one of Sister Sally,
bombs exploding and guns loading.
A boy –solitary, a scene of the country. -Welcome Home.

This lad grew up and became a Dad.
I am sure he was the happiest man I've ever known.
I knew him only for thirteen years-
I owe it to him for my life and what I am.
The war wounds caught up with him
prematurely, Jesus said, WELCOME HOME.

Home

For now the sweetness of fresh cardboard,
just for tonight is mine:
A can of lager,
a tired sleeping bag.
The Salvation Army bringing comfort,
a choice of soup or tea- with a smile.
A cigarette butt of a kind,
just manages to take away the memory of

the kettle boiling fiercely before the click.
Hot embers from coal fires,
babies crying.
The failure won't go away.
The thoughts mess with my head,
all day they natter at me;
a home, the past, and nasty things.

I'll make it on my own one day.
I will! With flowers that smell sweet.
Like the baby I held and heard its first cry.
But for now leave me
to rot here, with mates like *needle*…

Who does like waking in the dark?

Suburbia

Middle class houses
we rise above,
to PVC windows, 4 beds that detach us-
set us apart from the rest.
The lattice blinds close us in,
and keep others from seeing.
Classed as a better home.

We pay more for our beer
Wear good gear - with a designer name
We have a leafy park
Lights after dark
Pay more for our council tax.

This is happening everywhere,
in Kuala Lumpa, Greater London, Sweden and France.
Even secretly in Hong Kong and China, where people
love to dance to The communist air.

We help the burglar, who regularly
rides up and down our cycle paths.
We scrape to have a better deal than those urban kids
Who we share the same school with-
Or pay.
It's about able people doing their best.
Oh! and here the traffic is less.

Time has passed. We gained the pain.
There are smaller houses being built,
for sale on the street, at half the price;
for these unsustainable communities to buy.
Homes for all the one parent families-
Of wrecked lives re-housed.
Malvina Reynolds can write, a new song,
about her bourgeois conformist values.
As we face our utopia dreams alone.

Home is many things

A place where foreigners can stay
to help pay the bills. They learn English.
Two dogs to protect and play with two sons.
The going to work and school routine,
forgetting things even after reminders.
Check… the football kit, the duke of Edinburgh award scheme,
The extra class of IT, football.
The meeting after work,
that makes it difficult to pick the kids up.
Ring Helen again. NO! Well, perhaps Nan can.

The cleaner, the washing, the gardener needs paying,
The supervising, the pleasing.
Helen's Ewan coming for an exchange sleepless sleepover.
The dog has a cut foot, it needs nursing.
I am there helping- like a tool that fits many jobs.

The baffling day is nearly done-
Then the cooking and the coming together to eat.
Who likes this and who likes that?
Homework! 'Feet off the table please'.
Ah the weekend- The shopping, then, time off!
The kids to Dad's one weekend in two.

I go home to a tranquil place
where the garden is not massive;
and the washer is not always whirring
The TV is easy to watch;
not taken over by Wii and other stuff.
Baking- that pasty
only I and a chosen friend to eat them.

My lovely bed, instead of a bunk:
Not having to share a room
Not being disturbed in the night
with confused dreams.
I can do my favourite things like:
Work for the Red Cross
Read and write poetry
Go to gigs and workshops
Socialize with my circle of friends.

These soon get boring though
-especially when they don't turn up
because it's a cold day.
…Then the one line text saying
'come back Nan, we miss you'.
This sometimes saves the day.

Home Again

The smell of dough rising,
the china cups tinkling.
The kettle on the hob boiling,
the cake baking,
The family… all waiting.

The Church bells ringing,
Choir boys singing.
The mellow light bringing
him yearning
to see to see those faces smiling.
The banner waving
welcoming.

The dog barking,
when he sees who's walking
Up the pad, mum crying,
dad saying,
Bring out the fatted calf,
he's home again.
Who?... My lad.

Eggs in one Basket

I've found a cosy spot,
where I am warm and dry.
There are four wooden slats where,
I nestle in between
near where the green paint didn't reach.

The two windows beneath me,
they get battered on a windy day
by the Boston Ivy clinging.
The leaves are glossy, green, and strong-
 red when autumn comes.

Hiding away here, underneath the eaves,
I cannot be seen through the leaves.
Keeping these eggs warm is easy up here;
today they are breaking…

Guess what I've got?
Four mouths to feed.
Yellow beaks, chirping loudly.
I go to get the food
and hurry back alone…
this morning though-
I found a ladder resting right beside my home.
Oh! Pest! They're pulling the Ivy down.

For we are not alone

A broken heart is forever,
but I am not alone,
there is you
somewhere out there.
Why did you go? You didn't say.

I remember that you had many things to do,
one of them was leaving it all behind-
that's very hard to do!
I didn't know that you meant me.
I wonder if you are all alone?

I have our son,
he looks so much like you,
so I am not alone.
What do I say to him- about you though?

We will wait
until that day, when you need us more
than all the other distractions.
I will write to you, even though,
you never phone or send a message home.

I hope you find what you are looking for,
and that you are not alone.
All you left here, my love,
is waiting, growing stronger.

Now we are putting away the past,
leaving it all behind,
like you did,
for at last, we are not alone.

Dover

The sedate White Cliffs Hotel, with sun lounges,
terraces and sea view rooms,
grandly welcome the traveller and the holiday maker—
very few now, since the town has been attacked by the reveller
of society's progress planner and *architacked.*

Snargate Street, long gone to the hungry jaws
that gnarled, the beauty and the beast;
to feed the hungry lorries,
and give a commercial feast.
Fox's Bakery, where kids from the school across,
put pennies in the slot, for an iced bun,
or a liquorice stick.

The bookshop, where one could buy and read and see,
memories, of how things used to be.
Reynolds, next door, conveyed goods to and from the docks.
The market, all gone now washed ashore,
Nowhere to eat your plaice and Dover sole anymore.

Manchester

A sharp blue glass triangle, juts out,
flying across the road in true Armani style.
Ignoring the rich, red sandstone, building, standing aside,
displaying beauty, from more than a century
gone by.
A library, ornate with sunflowers-
heads resting high, on a stone sill, clinging on,
pride being paramount;
it has it's place
leftover from the slum clearance,
the shacks, warehouses, and dark factories.

Replaced, by young people and their urgent life.
Built out of need-
Buzzing, busy with businesses and flats.
The honey pours into the streets.
The festival stalls, offer, temporarily,
speciality foods, available permanently-
elsewhere in town.
The calypso sounds from centre stage-play
in rhythm, to people grazing patiently, like cows-
moodily standing or sitting on Sunday,
chewing the cud, of a regenerated town.

Seaside - a discussion is taking place…

It is not possible to be poisoned by food unless it is eaten,
otherwise-the temptation is in the eating.

At the boarding house of Mr and Mrs Albert,
in an unnamed holiday town, unmistakably England.
There are some red, blue, yellow
and white striped deck chairs in the park,
the cloths occasionally shaking, in the east wind.
The sun is shining through the sturdy wooden frames,
casting shadows on the tarmac near the grass,
sit empty until 3'o clock.
looking forward to the pavilion-
white, Victorian stone and cement
pillars stand, ornate, with carved pomegranates -
one Sunday afternoon in August.

A hand written billboard, brass drawing pins used to attach it
to the free standing wooden arch, inviting the brass band,
(who wear with pride) navy and red uniforms-
decorated with golden coloured epaulets,
showing they're the best band from miles around-
their conductor of renown. The cornet soloist reaches high,
the melodies are sweet -sweep tears from the eyes of yesteryear.
A gallop, a waltz, next a medley of the latest musicals.
A welcome for the stand-ins, from another band-
an e-flat bass and a trombone player.
The metal music stands with an insignia draped across,
the music sheets pinned down, while they blow.

Those without, make do with paper sun-hat, (busy with old news).
Trousers and sleeves rolled up, despite the sun and suit.
The enamel jug of tea and four pot cups, the ten shilling deposit
lost to a world of you do something to me; a clap.
The children play jacks- quietly on the grass.
They, listened to mamma say *not to eat it*,
pork pie is easy for the children to refuse though.
Another clap, this time, thunder ends the day.
They run for cover- dad, hardly able.
The band finishes hurriedly
with an excerpt from Handel's Water Music.

The tent

Blue is a mass, the sky, the sea,
the cloth over the altar.

It is in the warm, cool or cold
look in the eye that sees.

Blue is a hue at midnight,
calm and still, lying unclaimed.

Blue is, unusually,
what food supposedly is not.

It is God in me and me in God-
the spiritual colour of my destiny.

It is the new bruise before the old
-before the healing begins.

It is the whale and the mackerel scale
and the mackerel is me.

It is the sadness of the heart
when the blues music starts.

It is the tent I erected;
to protect me.

Tide

The foam,
soiled from the industry of the sea
spews and yawns back and forth
into the bay,
…crashing into the ravine
lined with high black rock.
Cliffs on either side.

The cove fills up ferociously.
The mussel pickers flee from the mud,
to the rusty steps quickly, to safety,
escaping, the greedy sand grabbing sea.
Soon the cove is full
and still;
a lone canoeist rows deftly.

The white lighthouse, stands tall.
Visitors run for their lives as the causeway
disappears, into the foaming monsters mouth.
Step by step,
the legs with rolled up jeans,
cling to black buckets, filled with pride,
wet and satisfied

head to the pub, pier,
or penny arcade.
Some will catch the last of the fishing light,
along the promenade wall;
baiting up in the green liquid sea.

The spider weaves a web
and waits patiently
for her prey
underneath the railings,
on the platform landing, several rusty steps,
where, worn enamelled notices, warn tourists
of the perils of the sea.

On the mud

Not huddled with others,
ready to go out to sea
as a pleasure boat,
or on tourist fishing days,
or even, a light oared rowing trip,
or races keen and strong.
Not painted brightly,
floating proudly,
ready to take on anything.

No! this is me, in my discarded state:
edges worn and crumbling,
unattractive, neglected, without oar,
leaning on the mud-
wanting so much to be needed;
or for Simon to wave,
I'd even listen to his friend, the one who talks a lot,
about, I don't know what,
wanting to claim the big catch
and set them free.

Men fishers

Pulling mackerel out of the sea,
blue, silver and slippery,
like trickles.

We fished on the other side,
our haul was overflowing.
Our bait was free.

The boat cocked when the shoal went by;
rods shaking as we pulled them in
5 or 6 at a time,

we were shaking too
with excitement.
They were thrown, scared,

into a communal bowl,
for us to prepare later.
taught by the seaman's skill

Anger

A few people swimming in the calm sea,
eerily, free from the warm wild day outside.

The restaurant shuttered, no activities,
a time to stroll and enjoy the beach.

Suddenly, a ten-foot wave reared up like an angry bull
raging, snatched me, and took me to hell.

Battered, face down- screwed into the muddy sand,
forced to submit to the madness of the sea.

A boat broke from its anchor point, pushed and mixed me
in the deluge of debris, that was up and down and all around

from the past. Swirling untamed, into hair and mouth,
seaweed tangled in clothes, dragging me along,

pushing my limp body towards the shore helplessly.
pants black with sand, grit and slimy things

noticeably, as the swell lifted me uncontrollably
another tidal force flung me, bashing me- to the liberty

of someone's outstretched arms; he managed,
I don't know how, to pull me to safety

comparative safety…

Walking on water

There is a storm at sea
this involves me
with my list of things to do
I can't get through-

but my priority is you.

Today I fed the five thousand:
and still had time to do for others
what you would have me do
even though they less deserved my time

more than you.

Then I walked on water
It was fine
till I saw your ghost
and then I sank,

you caught me and held me

in the nick of time
till I was able
with my good intentions
to cling to the boat

by my miraculous powers.

Poems of Love (I)

Persuasion

His voice, soft,

persuades my love, emerge! emerge!

No! stay sweet, and virgin like

so none can take, and give, that kind of love that danger

waits to kill.

Hurting now the soft voice says, Adieu!

And then the pulse fades-

It cannot live.

Poems of Love (I)

Uncompromised

There it is forever;

whole, unmovable, every sinew locked in,

all known morals set aside.

This is there, and does not compromise;

does not confide,

even to its own soul.

Does not make amends for anyone, or anything;

because love is- and reigns supreme.

Just one breath and it would awake- for goodness sake,

to perpetuate Its need to be.

Marching to Zion

I ought to be working, not dreaming,
staying up half the night scheming,
trying to conceive a plan,
that tomorrow will be thwarted again.

I ought to be decorating, not
solving problems that are fraught,
like, trying to do out my daughter's house;
it won't help *her*. I am here, she's just moved there.
We are miles apart.

I could be writing a letter.
Instead, I'm wasting my time
with riff raff thoughts.
So I stay awake and dream all night
I sleep in hell. I don't know why?.

I could be praying-
I care a lot for those who are awake like me,
Who don't know the answers
and have no one immediately, to whisper,
'come to bed don't bother your head
tomorrow's another day'.

I could be making a poem!
That would be better than being in a daze
till late, drinking the wine of wrath,
being concerned if I've got cancer or not-
and what to do if I have.

It's all better now. I made myself busy.
I found a book on the shelf about
'Chatsworth' where the bombs dropped
and how they re-built their church.
I thought at first it was the *big house* but it wasn't.

I read how these people laboured and toiled,
met with a plan
and suddenly, before all the finances were found,
before they began to get things off the ground,
they realised they had rebuilt that amazing church- within.

Morning

The bell tolls the parting.

In the morning
a different light:
roses glow virgin-like
feather soft and frail-
some vibrant
outside petals loose and light-
darker inside the moist tight bud-
some die.

Don't cry! or mourn too long,

the strong perfume
will last through to a new season,
in which we rejoice-
the same words will be sung again-
with different voice.

Help

You were the one that knew how;
the one who I can't stand to think of now.
because of
your success-
your diva ness,
your tendency to ignore me.
Your ability to cope
with your world, that is so big-
I can't make you happy.
Or give *you* what you want.

Sister you saved me, you took me
from the train that came crashing into my head.
Sometimes in a superstore
it wouldn't stop.
Day after day,
sometimes I screamed, anywhere!
walked the dog,
for hours and hours,
days. Sometimes
I stayed in bed.
I was captured.
For me the end had come.

Then that day you came to stay-
your love saturated me,
you said calmly,
go away, and it did.
You played a director on a film set:
You gave everyone a role.
(They enjoyed being led.)

You said to me, *breathe deeply*, and I did.
Then you said- when the train was on its way,
allow this to be, this is the one to fight.
You directed and produced
the right answer for me and my head.
You have given me your all.
You're:
all I need.

Words

Thank you,
I loved it; write,
if only for me.
Even if it is
far fetched and away from mind.

Trust,
it will go;
the wind will blow,
a bird will fly, the spirit will soar

in stillness,
somehow,
that word will be,
silently heard.

Poems of Love (II)

Love being processed

Kindle now the fire that slowly burns-
awaiting to be lit-
the passion hides,
this is how
I allow my love,
to live or die.
Otherwise it will be sold to slaves
not even masters know.
To lie alone, unknown and unidentified.
So I wait-
what sacrilege!

Poems of Love (II)

Love

And if I sigh,
I sense my heart is beating for the love
I told myself:
when inside I craved a space to link
my love forever, to understand him,
to give everything for love.
I, lie.

Fear penetrates my being-.
I am afraid to give
what I have-
in case then,
I am lost,
and left with nothing.
A coward's life I live!
Even though,
even I need nothing other than this.

Poems of Love (II)

Of Love

Keep it still, keep it quiet,
my love can easily be defiled.
The cuckoo moved, and the egg fell,
smashed and lay useless, a broken shell;
it would have flown, if in the night,
it could have grown,
and found strength to fly away.
It should have known.

Old Tree.

Old tree, tall, silky –
a figured hand
stripped bare of bark,
exposing the reality of age.
Moss clinging on one side of
each scrawny branch,
still reaching for the sky;
standing firmly on the ground.

Immersed in green flood light
in the dark night,
eerily waving,
silently
saying, so many different things-
through rain, snow, wind
and ages past.

Last night the golden dog fox
stood, awesome
by her side;
aligned, perched, on the seat that rests
in the moonlight.

The fall out

A banquet of a higher kind,
plenty to go round.
Published abroad on Sky TV,
everyone scrambling to see
what will this do for me?

Then the clearing up:
the sharing out
the forgotten toasts not meant
the dogs eating the leftovers.

Summing up it seemed to be:
money is blood, I mean my blood.
You have a choice- I didn't!
What do we do with it now?

Return to Ruskin

Hey!
I am returning to my seat of learning.
Wrapped up in my comfort zone.
My pillows full of duck down,
My nice bed, I will leave behind;
It doesn't bother me.

I have a few plots ready in my head,
So go on – let the music play,
I am prepared to begin
a shorter course at Ruskin.

Three days only though
Drama for the radio,
I will be good at that.
A year out is too long to be away.
I'm glad to revisit in the interim,
I'll be there when the chemo kicks in.
I'll be ok for this short time.
Hi! There, my lovely friends,
Caterers, tutors admin and Ed from the boat,
I'm coming back to learn
to be a genius
at Ruskin

Pass the parcel

It is me!
I have heard you,
I have heard you three times.
I'm ready at last.

I have seen all the hurt,
the wrongs and the rights
and all that has passed.

When you gave birth,
I heard your cry;
I saw suffering, with no gain-
  a baby without joy.

Clothes stained with blood
on children as men.
The evil and greed,
I have broken its back.

I am here to separate;
not to step this side or that.
I have come to lay down my Ebenezer.

Yes it is I!
I have heard you.
I will do what it takes-
to accept the hurt.
I will lay down the stone in my heart.

Oblivion

It is when nothing is left of what was
When 'no mans land'- comes to us.

When the nuclear bomb finally drops
And all that is dear to us is no more.

When the creator has turned His back on us
and we are deprived of awe.

That is when the weather is neither cold nor hot.
It is what those who do not believe have, when they die.

It is not being able to be persuaded,
not being thought about.

When there are no more babies
and no point in hoping.

No trees, no falling leaves, no colour.
It is when the big light goes out.

When the abomination of desolation
is here, clear, not in the pages now.

Making amends

I came across an ark,
it was upside down-
life's like that.

It bobbed around
on the cusp of the wave;
it looked like I was drowning.

I called the lifeboat men, they came
in their small blue and white craft,
sunshine yellow, storm proof coats.

They rescued the ark, it fell right side up,
eventually I went inside;
it was much bigger than it looked.

There was someone who served me
hot sweet tea, bread and honey
who said softly, *welcome.*

I smiled,
he gently untangled the olive branch from my hair.
It came away so easily.

Marking time

Eleven strokes.
The sun constantly shines.
Bring out the dead.
The deadness is discarded;
the beauty gone for a while.
The seeds sown again by the earth eye.

By bird,
by wind,
and fallen rain water.
That which lies hidden in the dead,
is sewn in resurrection promise

to be glorified
by a miracle-
there is certainty all around,
when the clock ticks on
and the bell tolls- if not for you.

Made to Measure

Now that we have found you- we can't let go.
You are super professional people, who work for
Management Pro.

Who's that in the black Paul Smith tie?
The date last night was just a fight;
you need the time to put it right.

The Prada Gal, she's looking good,
(look at the heel on that shoe!)
Did you know your husband needs you too?

Is the balance right?
Then, you can be a plant in this super company.
Your growth will flourish-and the reward is this-

you are special people with a mission,
you are the chosen few,
and the target is- with passion.

Bling! Bling! here we go
here's a challenge …make this company grow.

Fasten your seat belts and go with the flow-
flying high.

as we dip down, Bora Bora waits
Bling! Bling! here is Space, The terrace…

we are the super beings out to catch a few rays.
Keep it going - Make that company grow.

Poems of Love III

Might it not be there…?

I left my heart open to the ravages of time and,

Became insecure.

Unsure of being sold to love's untimely slight, when all at once,

I felt it might not be true.

Could I stand the hurt if it were not so?
Even though I know, that in my heart, it happened, and this is true…

Partly because

Partly because I saw this girl

- And I don't know what to do,

Partly because I feel so good,

That I'm asking you;

I don't want to scare her at all.

Partly because *I* am scared

That it won't work out right.

Partly because she looks alright.

Oooowwch

Three of four then it don't hurt any more.

The first is the one you remember again and again.

And dream- when things go wrong

That, you would have been better to stick to it then.

You still think of that love,

But it is not as it seemed

At the time when you were besotted and young,

When you thought that your prince had come.

But really! Did you forget?

He married that other one.

Father's day. I was thirteen

When his clock stopped at 11p.m-
the next morning he died,
I was sent to Grandma's out of the way.
No one told me, but I knew he'd died.

Her apron was clean and fresh;
she hugged me, when I came home.
I ran upstairs. He was covered over,
a handkerchief tied round his face.

He was cold like smooth stone.
So that's what Mrs Duffy did to you while I was away.
How did he go, what did he say?
Apparently! 'the gates of heaven are open.'

The surgeon pushed him away.
Told her what he had to say;
mum and I brought him back home,
to suffer and die…

my angel said *don't go to school today*
go home, on that Friday before he died.
He wanted pineapple- so I biked 7 miles and got a tin.
He couldn't eat it though.

I had been potato picking, for the money.
I bought him five Robin and a Mirror,
stayed with him and read it through. In a way
it was a dark happy day.

Just three months before, he was fishing at Wainfleet,
he camped, I heard him singing and playing his banjo
in the pub. I looked through the window.
He didn't catch many fish though.

How did he manage to learn so much?
He never went to school: he was an artist,
a builder, a teacher, a musician, a gardener,
a craftsman of embroidery, carpentry and mending shoes.
I can go on.

A gassed and shell shocked soldier hero,
relic of World War I. Long gone -what a life he led!
What a beacon in mine! Whatever I do now,
always involves him in someway, somehow.

The atomiser

I feel spiritual when I spray
the contents of a bottle
that Ruth gave me,
she is kind.

It releases a myriad
of memories:
the woodland
where I picked cold bluebells
on a hot day.

the smell from the leather
dad hung outside to dry
preparing to mend our shoes.
the Sunday lamb
with mint
I cut and chopped
and put vinegar and sugar in.

the sorrel flower-
that reminds me of
the abbey where the monks live;
(my great grandfather is buried there)
where I went to mass.
I saw the nativity set before the altar.
where dad prayed steadfastly.
there was the smell of incense
the softness of the Holy water
that touched my skin.

the atomizer sending
the finest droplets to my face
tenderly, like a kiss before I go
and pace the day
in peace.

The Rape

I grapple with the image
you passed on to me;
it took you three years to test me-
that's not long, since you held it for thirty three.
Did it matter if no one knew it
from your point of view?

The day you went to see your mother
in pieces.
On the floor, dead
flesh hanging from the ceiling,
chopped up,
slung in the pantry and in the hall,
blood splattered on the step,
on the door handle.
The toppled over cup.
Her clothes in a pile.

I see your face, ravishing
the time it took to tell me.
The wall you leaned on outside the scene
holds me up.
The vomit you left there:
became the job you lost,
the marriage,
the three year old boy.
Your place in society changed
to a murdered mother's son.

I have seen you rob and cheat;
hating people,
guarding everything you own
from them.
I have seen you locked up
because of it.
I see you alone with the crowd selling gold.

Today I have seen a light in your eyes;
you gave that image to me
I have seen you set free.

Are we really worth more than these?

'Turn around when possible!'
I needed to go back
to that little thing I had left
behind, without a mother;

she fluttered behind a plant pot,
refusing to drink out of fear.
It was worth so much more than two farthings
I was sure; with its yellow breast.

It had gone. I looked in other places,
no signs of who had come to the rescue,
or what the cat had done!
More to the point- what *I* had done!

At night in the glare of the security light;
(still on my mind,)
I checked the pot again. I saw a yellowish thing,
that moved, I discerned two long legs.

Stooping to see if the fledgling had returned.
The thing suddenly jumped up at me,
we almost kissed,
I will never know why a frog was there.

Memories too hard to memorise

I'm left with memories
I cannot stand to memorise
even the happy ones
when me and the kids played footie on the lawn.
Joe taught me superb football skills and tricks with the ball.
'Nan's good' he said,
James just laughed 'Yeh! Right,' he led me
by the arm, to see his rabbit.

The rabbits were taken to a barn,-
there were two.
The fish were given away to-
I don't know who.
I took the toys, to a car boot
for other boys,
Jackie had the food,
her four would devour that and more.

And their school! That had to go too,
no more Catholic ballyhoo,
or open days when I was proud
to gaze at school plays;
and think that only *I* had Grandsons.

Yesterday, when I packed
away some old cards-
I found the one they'd sent to me-
and there it is again tears in my eyes.
How can I be glad and wish them well
When I am going through hell?
-they must be too,
sometimes we do these things though.

I'm all at sea

When I'm at sea in the rocky boat.
I feel sea-sick.
I see a killer whale's tail in front of me
frightening and awesome.
I can see all this, it is big and true and real.
What I can't understand is-that man

hiding under the fig tree
out of the sun,
thinking someone's chasing him,
or, why he went on that boat
and played all those people up
who he knew. They feared for their lives.

Then throwing himself overboard.
Diving out of the way again.
He spent three days inside for that.
Finally he jumped out onto the beach.

Taking it from there, some time later...
we meet the real man on the sands,
who cooked us some fish.
after spending 3 days inside.

The things that broke the silence

Lying outside on the grass.
Hoping for peace, but there were:
car horns repeatedly honking,
car doors shutting, slamming,
people chattering, shouting to each other.

A loud clock striking eleven without cause
not like the bells that tolled
reminding me of not going to church.
A jet plane leaving a long vest of smoke behind
and my head, whirring around.

I couldn't hear the gentle brush of the dry grasses
wafting to and fro with the soft breeze
that took away silently the heat of the exposed sun.
Or the swallow slipping elegantly
over the tall trees, rustling their leaves.

The last call of the blackbird! I hardly heard at all.
I didn't hear the discarded fledgling feather-
trapped between a clover leaf; lying-
not belonging there, I didn't hear it squeak,
or tell me a message that the bird had flown.

I didn't hear the spider scurrying on my hot skin-
without a cause.
compete with him and his eight legs-
I wouldn't dare,
so I gave him the brush off.

Sleeping objects lying around

It was there, still in the box.
I rediscovered my memory.
The satin cover slid down, like a peach silk negligee
and fell to the floor.
Fell to the floor, slippery.
I remembered the
fountain of blue fluid,
flowing through 22 carats.

He held it, caressed it, and used it to make a contract,
Not to expect much more than death,
I signed it too.
We held it, caressed it, and used it to make a contract.
The tawny tourtashell body, smooth and slender,
held tightly by the gold band
which bound us perfectly.

However long we were drawn apart:
we would gravitate back to each other.
The golden arrow pointed
like it was Cupid's own;
pierced,
placed and claimed them- unconditionally.
I remembered his lips, soft like butter-
fondling and gently kissing and sucking;
sometimes making a noise
as he thought carefully and sighed.

It was hooked on his breast pocket.
I gently took it away and returned it,
to mine.
I put it next to the heart,
where it beats in time endlessly.

If I were called in

If I were called in to build a church
I would bring in Jesus
I would ask Him to turn over the tables
and take away the hard wooden pews.

My litany would be
taken over by miracles.
I would ask what He means
by us doing more than Him.

Instead of taking the offertory
I would give my soul for free
going to church for me would be something
like home; where we look in the mirror and frown.

I would ask if we can take away the
Sabbath and make it your own,
your day, everyday.
I would fly the flag at half-mast
He will know when I ask Him
to give us more time to let Him in.

Notes written up in 2008 waiting for the 187th hospital appointment.

Written into a poem in July 2010

Making notes drive away the tense feelings.
I write in an agitated way
in the waiting room of the 'Wellcome Clinic'
Me, bringing the effects of my third session
of Capecitabine.
One day they will look back and wonder
who dared to give this out.

Burning you up from the inside out.
Legs, feet and hands blistered,
heartburn, eyes watering, limping like Hiroshima victims.
Volunteers, now their husbands have gone,
handing out icy drinks of water
to those who can't help themselves.

They shout, next, then say your name out loud.
Please help to transform the strangeness!
Where God is listless and Angels fear to tread.
I sit here amongst the dead.
In the corridor next door
where white walls and thin beds, wait.
I am tired of treatment.

I am waiting to begin
an undecorated medical calendar:
I want a life! A life! life!
I see a navy coloured board
with a yellow arrow on it,
it speaks to me: more than black and white
it says WAY OUT
that's me, I'm going.

Notes from the 187th hospital appointment

Violent storms
pouring out of spirits
from cold and forlorn lips
erupts tense moments unexplained
waiting with head bowed,
as if uninterested.

The rain descends
begins to cleanse
the tree of life
lightening and thunder claims
a small chance of life and momentarily
chases each doubt across a darkened sky.

A step towards immortality

It is in the tears of the adieu
That the mortal in us wakes.
When saturated love has almost turned to pulp-
We must find the courage to release the pain and move on again.

Needs must, or else bewitched by unrequited agony,
we begin to live in the realms of misery,
holding our weakness in time passed by.
Laurels spent, games played and lost.

Taking our joy, bliss, memories and sweet experience,
Not relived
Like a leaf dying in the rain.
Or wallowing in a time that has ended, been and gone.

To begin in trembling fervour,
progress, build again in fresh green pastures.
Deliver anew. (albeit in retrospect of time past);
Into bravely conquered virgin grass.

Then when age comes, we do not linger
when our time has come,
we know then it is truly time to move on;
our life now has just begun.

The Wilderness

Zoom in
on little drops of silver and gold
on the carpet of grass.
Lie or walk with the wealth of one tiny head
or the multitude

Forty white petals with brightness
for each day of darkness.
One perfect Son, in the form of a flower.
the image is ours.

Or see the yellow eye of forgiveness
watching over the wilderness.
Where we fast ourselves
of love, joy, and peace.

We, regarding our long days in solitude,
as martyred.
Like where no one went before.
Compare our suffering!
Surely we wouldn't dare!

We, being tempted to die and fall;
hearing words we cannot bear
to speak to anyone about.
What they know, I am
and only I know what has to be done.

The chains wrapped around me
to secure me in my dungeon,
will fall off.
When my head is ready
to break free;
and my heart fit to speak.

What the sun brings out

I was walking by the river;
So were many others.
The sun made the walk pleasant.
Ladies slipper slipping over the other side,
  if flowers go there?
Birch trees, tall, loosing their silver coating,
leaning awkwardly with the weight.
Families walking, making flashes
of sun happen with the trees and spaces.
The mallards with the head- under- wing- syndrome.

A family man serving a crying baby in a pushchair.
He poured orange juice from a carton into a baby bottle.
He becomes harassed-
the orange juice squirted over his nice white t shirt;
You could see him get angry at himself.
He was trying to pacify the infant – without success.
That man could cut down a fifty-foot birch tree,
(with or without a harness), using a chain saw-
Make the wood into a hundred logs
for next years winter's fires
and still not make his t-shirt dirty
Both jobs need doing though.

My mystery man

My mystery man
who's seen darker days,
no more now though; all
gone with chalky,
one above them all.

He treads on my feet
wanting to do Mrs Dalloway's party.
He sails with Conrad on the seas;
don't go before you were mine please.

When he finally comes to cook
in my kitchen
I will wipe his feet with myrrh,
even though he treads on mine

I will always do worse than her.
So richard or nick whatever he believed
I am a vegan
didn't mean to deceive
what will you do now, please?

Space

Apex chimney-stack warm
from last nights log fire
four stone colonnades stand on tiles
shining with a dusky hew
pink daisies grow from troughs in the stone wall

Mediterranean pan tiles cover the roof of the next floor down
where the pool sparkles cold
pine trees wake in the promising sun
from past winter days, shuddering in the breeze
discarding the last few fledgling cones

down through the grey gliding automatic gates
moving in the 2x4
down towards the salt flats
leaving behind Puig Gruos and hills
lush, on a February day

where doves coo
and palm trees reach in diverse ways
burdened by their heavy ochre fruit
the banana plant lurks beneath
the bird of paradise points the way

from either side the road, the garners yield
the pregnant salt pans piled, paused
expecting to be exported
by the boat moored ready
to sail the silver sea.

Last Goodbyes

Working so hard to finally say 'that's done'
medicals, visas, a thousand and one
jobs gradually get you there.
Courage, born out of fear,
and you say 'jobs a good un'
and go, without a tear.

The bedding washed, the t-shirts, pants,
towels still wet from the morning shower.
All the odd socks picked up washed and paired,
the abandoned teddy and the Lego bits.
No more shouting, laughing, crying,
no home now, and soon…

the house cleaned and almost ready,
for another host to move in and make it their domain.
The car- not needed now, just fits in the garage
amongst the storage, packed to the roof
with unwanted things
left behind for me to mind and maintain.

Friends think it's great what she's done.
'Yes she is brave' I think.
The light fades and the heart begins to sink,
she's in the air now.
O God, grant them safety.
When will I see them again?

The captive

extended from the kitchen floor
- a flagstone
amongst many more
strayed towards the hall and door;
they bore a shiny finish
of red and greying streaks.

she stepped and trod carefully,
stiletto, strife, forked,
she trod
between the concrete edge;
-then, one foot on tip toe
cast a shadow over all her life.

he, lay and bled-
it had carried no one dead before
the knife went in
tears and pain begin
to scream again…again…

he died-
and she, ran along the slippery stone
to her liberty:
she had never seen the light of day:
it blinded her eye,

frightened her heart
told her not to stay
in her own environment

Do they know what,
she did ?

The rooftops

It was a safe place to have the meeting,
on the coping stones,
the cowl,
the TV aerial,
and the sky dish.
They had an agenda about SAD and about SUN.
I could hear them reading it out
and discussing it. There was a lot of fuss

They circled around a bit and conferred,
then they were gone,
the blackness
lifted like a blanket.

All *their* chicks had flown the nest
like mine;
so *I* have nothing better to do now,
than go and find a place in the sun.
Now my chicks have flown and I'm alone-

anyway I can't go on my own.

All is safely gathered in

Suspended under the birch tree- a bouquet of gnats,
gallivanting, flit blindly,
darting in and out
and through the last, bright early evening rays.

A few yellow leaves fall,
turning round and round, slowly,
twirling gently to the ground;
stacking up like casino chips- making rich.

Ants run furiously up
the sticky bramley tree, in harmony,
bringing the aphids back along the branch,
to their garner ceremoniously.

Eaking now each minute of the light,
the white waffle clouds- served on a powder blue plate,
feed the farmer and the ant their needs,
till, the orange table cloth is shaken and all the work is done.

Moving On

There comes a time when it is time to move on
…and do what has to be done.

A time when one might feel
we no longer stand for what is real
in others eyes, and most of all –our own.

The clutter that was so intense
has brought a heavy load, dumped it and gone.
...it's easier said than done-

excuses just resound,
now you see that if you're brave,
you go to where the light shines

or the grave waits
and you are buried alive,
not cherished for your life's sacrifice.
.
The truth always seems obscure
and some times the awakening comes in a series
of devastating blows that are hard to take.

For goodness sake hold on!
Let the truth stare you in the face
and push and shake you out

into the rapids that take you
where the current flows
and you are glad to be alive.

Opportunities pose
and what you thought might be a problem once,
well, today isn't, because *you* won.

Further acknowledgements

You me and a dog named Blue

You in your small corner and I in mine

Joy

Business as usual

submissions incorporated in The Selston Parish Anthology
November 2010

Haiku

Reindeer Writer's Newsletter
November 2010

Nasturtiums and the Bumblebee

Reindeer Writers News Letter
September 2010

Keeping Warm and a poem called e.on

(extracts taken from 'What did I eat today?' a book by Kathleen Bartholomew

'The Southwell Folio'a cultural community magazine. Issue No 4
July/Aug 2010

A Festive Feast (poem) " "Issue No 6 Oct/Nov 2010

Dover

Forward Press, Remus House Coltsfoot Drive

Northampton PE2 9JX

Anthology entitled 'Inspired Minds'
July 2010

The best way to spend your holiday kids

Anthology Happily 'Ever After'
January 2011

On Dover Beach

Anthology 'Under Salt Sky'
January 2011

Love's Elergy

Anthology 'A Piece of My Heart'
January 2011

You in your small corner and I in mine...short story

Reindeer Writers News Letter
June 2010

The Spiritual Birth

Included in Church of Christ Magazine

Mary Scrimshaw Church of Christ Portland Road Selston Notts
April 2010

Last Goodbyes

Forward Press, Remus House, Woodston, Peterborough PE2 9JX

Anthology entitled 'Far and Wide' 31st May 2010

Begin Again

Forward Press, Remus House, Woodston, Peterborough PE2 9JX

Anthology entitled 'My Words Are My Voice' 31st December2009

Tide

Forward Press Remus House Woodston, Peterborough PE2 9JX

'Anthology entitled The Chessboard of Life' 31st October 2009

Hallowe'en Twins

Poetry Now, Woodston Peterborough PE2 9JX

Anthology entitled 'United In Words' 29th July 2009

Captive in Derbyshire

Poetry Now, Peterborough

Anthology entitled 'Awakening Inspiration'

(scheduled for publication) 31st January 2009

Moving On

Sheltered Times Ashfield District Council

Urban Road, Kirkby in Ashfield Notts
October 2008

Poesie De Paris

Poetry Now, Peterborough,

anthology entitled- 'Déjà vu'. 30th April 2007

Our Kid

Anchor Books, part of Forward Press. Woodston

Peterborough PE2 9JX

anthology entitled- 'Leader of the Pack- Animal Antics'.
November 2007

Might It Not Be

Poetry Now, subsidiary of Forward Press

Woodston Peterborough PE2 9JX
October 2006

Included in -

'Midland and East Anglia Poets'

(part of Forward Press), Woodston Peterborough PE2 9JX

24th November 2006

Welcome Home

Poetry Now,

part of Forward Press. Woodston Peterborough PE2 9JX

anthology entitled 'Poppy Fields'
September 2007

I'm Lost

Dogma Publications, editor Amanda Read

ISBN 978-1-84591-18-1

anthology entitled -'Shattered Illusions' 7th April2006

Childlike

Dogma Publications, editor Amanda Read

ISBN 1-84591-010-9

4 Overstrand Close, Bicester, Oxon OX26 4YP

anthology entitled 'Rhyme and Reason' 30th September2005

Death Came

United Press Ltd. London, EC1B 1JB

anthology entitled 'Body and Soul' 29th November 2005

www/unitedpress.co.uk/

Uncompromised

Exile, 'Poems to print'

John Marr, Exile, 8 Snow Hill, Clare, Suffolk. 16th December 2004

Biographical note about Kathleen Bartholomew

I began studying a degree course in English Literature and Creative Writing at Ruskin College Oxford in 2006.

I learned so much in my first year at college. I was told by one of my tutors I was a natural born poet. Compliments are scarce in that high standard educational environment; this spurred me on to do more and experiment with style and voice in the poetry I write- the rest is history. I had to leave Ruskin due to illness.

I work hard on my writing. I do poetry gigs every week at my local pub, at group meetings, or anywhere when I am invited to recite my poems.

I have also written a novel about living a life through the window of my cancer experiences. Look out for it: *What did I eat today?*

I think I will keep on writing forever, I am hooked.

This collection, *Moving On,* has been compiled from poems I have written over the last three or four years. I hope it encourages people to get over obstacles that life throws our way and move forward to a better life.

Index of Poems

www.ingramcontent.com/pod-product-compliance
Ingram Content Group UK Ltd.
Pitfield, Milton Keynes, MK11 3LW, UK
UKHW020202200726
13856UKWH00003B/1139

9 781446 724460